For Cathy,
with Thanksgiving
that you also
make your
home in
union.

HOME
BY
ANOTHER
ROAD

Fondly,

Cathy

march 2021

CATHY WARNER

Anna's Bay Books

Cover photo by Cathy Warner

And having been warned in a dream not to return to Herod,
they left for their own country by another road.
~Luke 2:12

For my husband Kevin
and my soul sisters Becky and Tarah
as we journey together for life

CONTENTS

SETTING OUT

WELCOME

Welcome the beautiful, sparkling, bright
expansive, shiny, easy, new, perfect, wonderful.

Welcome the old, battered, dusty, familiar
well worn, comfortable.

Welcome the challenging, unlovely, curmudgeonly
chipped, broken, lopsided, falling apart.

Welcome the hazy future, the cloud of unknowing.
Welcome the storm with its opportunity for soaking
the chance to be drenched in understanding.

Welcome to surrender as it scrawls
across the sky, a message in flaming clouds.

Welcome the uncertainty of where you will
lay your head, on which lilies of the field
you will fall beside at the end of the day.
Welcome spinning and not spinning, toiling and rest.
Welcome being arrayed in glory.

Welcome the breath deep into your scarred
and beloved body, and let that breath take you
below the consciousness of your own physical self.

Welcome the obstreperous obstructionists
and the ones trapped in their own trappings.

Welcome the motley crew, the saved and the sinners
the sweet soul and sick one, for they exist within you.

Welcome the log in your eye, the speck in your sister's

and every egomaniacal consumer-driven impulse
that has flicked to life in your mind, sleeping or waking.

Welcome them through your threshold, seat them in an armchair
by the fire; pour a cup of tea and serve it with all the care
and sweetness they so desperately crave.

And then dear one, dear self, dear God-flamed coal
ease their stories from their mouths.
Welcome the words as they tumble from dark cells
and sinews into the air, into the light.

Welcome them out of closets, basements, and skeletons.
Welcome them to become what they will—wisps of memory
holy and transparent, or muscle and skin.

Welcome what has come to be birthed or die in your arms
cradle the charred remains, or open a window
and welcome the flight into the future.

You cannot know, you never could, what might become
of you or anything you have ever loved. It might be alive
pulsing within you this very moment.

What else is there to do but open your eyes
and unstop your ears, lower your guard, drop
your jaw in wonder and let welcome permeate
your pores until you are nothing but a shimmering beacon.

Welcome, welcome, dear one.
It is good to have you here, at home.

ROUGH ROADS

YOU DO NOT HAVE TO BE GOOD

You do not have to be good.
You do not have to walk on your knees
for a hundred miles repenting.
—Mary Oliver

But that's what I want you to do—
crawl across the desert to my door
your knees bloody, your lips cracked.
Fall at my feet, grovel while I glare.

Prove to me, every day in every action
for the rest of your wretched life
that you are tormented and miserable
aware of exactly what you did
(every detail) to betray me.
Your sin unpardonable
one more thing I will not forgive.

You can try though, to eek mercy from me.
I will stand vigil at my door
cool glass of water in my grasp
shading my eyes with my hand
watching you scrape toward me.

You, hungering for benediction
thirsting for a blessing—
you will walk on your knees
repentant for a lifetime.

CRAZY ALONG HIGHWAY 9

She steps, swaying and strong
along the winding ribbon
of highway that threads
these mountain towns together.

She wears patchwork
skirts, faded boots
and an unstitched expression.
Today a teddy bear swings
in her grasp marking the seams
of miles raveled by.
Last week, she basted
a quilted rabbit to her chest.

She sings sometimes, lullabies
to mend her threadbare friends
as she traces patterns
from selvage to fold.
She doesn't see me or hear
the traffic weaving by.

She is happy, her self gone
to the dancing place.
And I wonder how many steps
until I join her.

THE IMPOSTER

The imposter talks like a professional
acts like she knows what she's doing
looks competent and calm gets results…

No one would guess she's floundering
vigilant and wary as though everyone
is poised to pounce at her slightest misstep
ready to belittle every mistake.

She hears their voices in Greek chorus
a never-ending refrain of "not good enough"
every time she undertakes a job
protocol, procedure she feels ill-prepared for.

It's exactly the way she learned to swim
arms peeled from around her father's neck
as he tossed her off the diving board
stood smiling while she sputtered
and slapped her way to safety.

As if near drowning builds strength
of character and more confidence
than sitting in the shallow end
buoyed by a lifeguard with a soothing
voice and steady hand.

Finally, the imposter has learned to reach
for the phone, a friend, a life vest
when flummoxed, anything sturdier
and stronger than her own ego.

CHRISTMAS DINNER

The suicide survivor, cancer patient, destitute,
alcoholic, and judgmental overachiever gather
not at a soup kitchen, not recipients of charity
just a fractured family reunited one night only.

Candied yams offered to the slurring one
whose odor overpowers the aroma of turkey
a tall glass of iced tea stirred for the one
brought back to life after an overdose
pillows plumped for the octogenarian
ensconced in a wheelchair tubed to oxygen.

All of us are weary of life's demands
and always we fall—
off the wagon, off our meds
off the charts, short of expectations.

A child is born this day come, as some believe
to save us—something we cannot seem to do
for ourselves or for each other.

Still we send our mumbled prayers clattering
among heaped platters serving kindness
along with cranberries and King's Hawaiian rolls
for our turkey and dressing communion.

The scattered body and blood are melded
in this meal as hand-over-hand hand-in-hand
forgiveness—deserved or not—is poured out
like gravy over mashed potatoes.

ABSCISSION

Leaves sloughed from the Japanese maple
in earnest the day she learned he was in
the ICU under sedation and restrained.
They fluttered to the ground
in bright blazing glory, serrated edges
spinning knifelike toward her heart
while she raked up the mess.

The next ten days he was tethered to bed
in a high-rise hospital near the highway
where trees gave way to strip malls.
There in California's Gold Country
the landscape beaten brown, evergreens
parched as his soul, everything was battered
brittle by the years'-long drought.

Every day of his confinement a new
question blew through her mind:
Would he regain consciousness?
Would he have brain damage?
Would he be able to care for himself?
Would his needs fall to her?

The next storm finally released
all the leaves from her backyard maple.
She gazed at bare branched beauty
knowing what to expect come spring—
buds and new life, nature's
uninterrupted resurrection story.

But staring at him the future
was murky. Each time he surfaced
hallucinations set him screaming
pummeling; the overdose still flowing
like sap through his capillaries.

The yard and his life both burst into flame
that fall bleeding bright, demanding attention
and with their fervent descent she saw
her hopes decay like once vibrant leaves
spent in wet heaps on asphalt.

She couldn't help but crush
the sodden pile with her tires
driving from home to hospital
and back, unable to escape
worst-case scenarios and tears
that settled on her face like mist.

All she wanted was a tidy yard
but desire snaps like twigs
in the face of destruction.

A week later his hospital bed
like her maple finally stood empty
discharged, but the restless wind
whipped and frenzied fir needles
tracked wherever her soles stepped
indicting every move she took
as everyone braced for the worst
helpless against the weather.

AVALANCHE

In Memory of Paul Imrie

I dream of climbers traversing yawning crevasses of ice
gingerly crossing ladders flung across glacial flow.
They wait at middle camp while blood oxygen doubles
then assault the east face. Ribs crack and lungs burn.

May's peak opportunity disappears beneath
hundred mile an hour winds. Bodies lie frozen.
Everest will not give them up.

Snow blows off the escarpment, an avalanche threatens
and the telephone rings. Out of the storm I climb breathless.
Answering, I hear a tearful voice:
This random flow of life has taken you at eighteen.

I remember you at eight, quiet in your valley of sadness
and watched as over the years you shed that weight
your smile growing as you travelled further into the distance
scaling landmarks until yesterday.

Yesterday you fell off a cliff, and today I am frozen
feet planted in ice.

I have only "I'm sorry." Two words, too hollow
too shallow to restore the one step you missed
the one step off the sheer wall that ripped the world open
when they found you wedged between tree and mountain face.

Today my lungs burn with grief as those who love
you stumble down the precarious steps through mourning

hating the cliff that claimed you now frozen in youth
and the word *Accident* that splatters headlines.

The world will think you reckless like the fools
who pay to summit inhuman landscapes. But I know
a different story. You were simply walking in the woods
that skirt your backyard after school with friends
alone only a few minutes when you fell.

You were just a boy doing what boys do: growing, surviving
even thriving. And now...we must learn to live without you
because God, like Everest will not give you up.

ECLIPSED

There's something about the lunar eclipse
when everyone steps outside to marvel
at the shadow that blocks her light.
They see our world in blackness define what's hidden
and the ribboned slip of bright peeking out
from Luna's edges that Earth can't quite eclipse.

Minutes and hours later his shadow is gone
and the moon comes back to herself
reflecting, always reflecting, another's glow.

But nobody watches the moon in ordinary time
when she pushes tides in ebb and flow
waxes and wanes in a dance she alone choreographs.

No one saw her follow you bright in your rearview mirror
as you drove away with just a suitcase
because his shadow was too big and too black.

Only the moon understood how peeking out from the edges
of your life lasted for years until you couldn't
see light around corners anymore.

Nobody pays attention on the ordinary nights
after you've been eclipsed. No one hears the car sputter
and the engine die or the door creak when you push
it open and stand silhouetted in the cold.

Only you look into the sky on a plain gilded night
to find your bearings. You align yourself with
different stars this time around—and the new moon
she waxes bright beckoning you.

A Lament for the Severed One

Let me gather the ragged
edges of your wound
bind it using school scissors
and scotch tape a child's tools
plied by a Girl Scout earning
another badge for her sash
as I obey the promise "to help
other people at all times."

But really what help is
my mediocre mending?
Band-Aid for a broken bone.
And for your Great Severing?

I have nothing....

I could scour the landscape
for your lost limb and finding it
I could clean, wrap, and return it
but for what purpose?
To be carted alongside as you limp?

You are split and I am torn.
Do I dig a grave for what you've lost?
Do I bury it and mourn, keep vigil
in the wet grass tears bleeding
in the dew as I weep over the tombstone
I've erected while you yet live hobbled
by violence?

I'm haunted by my failure
shamed because I should fix
it, you, everything.

Your spirit starves while my guilt
grows fat like a calf I should slaughter
at the altar, a plea for miraculous
reattachment of all that's been rent from you
an offering to assuage my complicity
my fear of collapse should I
come close enough to bear
the weight of your suffering.

THAT OLD COAT

The moments come without warning:
I'm yanked from my authentic skin thrust
back into old behaviors as quickly
as throwing on a vintage coat I wore
down with worry; a garment so familiar
it took decades to notice its ill-fit. I kept
shrinking to accommodate the cloth
so long outgrown it became a straitjacket.

It seems every time a storm brews I reach
for that moth-eaten coat the one I struggle
to make fit the one that shields me only
from what I need most in such circumstances:
the felt knowledge of my true self.
Instead, my contortions obscure the light
that shines within my own bones.

When the day turns harsh and cold
when I shiver and shake and the ache
for familiar fabric overcomes me I slap
my own hand away from the fraying collar
wagging fingers at my weakness when I ought
to hold out my hands soft, beckoning
those life-long worries pocketed
in my worn-out coat. If I kept calm, perhaps
I could lift the dead weight from my shoulders
cut it up for cleaning rags, find new purpose.
Then, the past just might stop chafing me.

REST STOP

THE INSOMNIA POEMS

One: The Point of Insomnia

The creative mind lit up can't turn off.
With my head on the pillow narrative spins itself
furiously and when I finally sit up, the vertical motion tips
the thoughts and the elegant arrangement
of words—so poetic and powerful in imagination—
into a jumble on the floor of some obscure lobe.

Insomnia–the ancient response I've inherited
from my mother and the line of ancestors before her
who crawled under furs on fourteen-hour nights
suspended in a twilight state in those pre-electric
days, restless bodies turning slowly like meat on a spit
thoughts knitting an alternate reality just below
the surface of consciousness.

My nocturnal brain fires when I take to my bed
like a hard-wired generator in an electrical outage
blazing light behind my eyes powering a city
of thoughts, wasted for decades before I knew
I could write, and those years when I thought
I should write but was too exhausted by mothering,
and those years when I resisted for no good reason
until I was whittled down by half-sleep and nightmares
into the sharp point of a pencil scribbling furiously.

Two: A Poem Before Sleep

Something lurks green and fecund
below daytime awareness—
the dark tiredness of almost sleep
when reality makes a shift and another layer
of consciousness is exposed.
For centuries we have wormed our way
there—beating drums, drinking potions
smoking substances, popping pills
all of it to transport us to the place
where the body becomes only breath
where pain and sensation mottle and muddle
into the background while the mind expands—
every thought endlessly fascinating.

But I feel them still, my aching muscles
that will not unclench, will not release their grip
on what they contain and protect, the secret
slipping of cells they will not allow.
They remember like elephants—they manifest
the pain body, the tension that has not evaporated
but has burrowed deep, a hidden incarnation
that does not relax despite self-revelation.

How I wish instead of this muscle-guarding
that there was a poem lodged between
my shoulder blades.

Three: The Liminal Edge

Walk this liminal edge of sleep
and it will lead you deftly
into a poem as if it were
the path into the woods.

You clutch at a basket—
words to deliver to your grandmother
who crossed an ocean and half a continent
waiting for you with her old language
a foreign tongue still friendly
in her mouth after eighty
long years here.

The words glow, as enticing
to the pioneer as indoor
plumbing and electric lights.
It takes a generation or two
or three to taste and see
to speak what has become of them.

The brave, the foolhardy
and those whose tongues bleed
from all they could not say
step into the boat
and press on with the stroke
of genius, the pull of oars.
And so, we sail, pens in hand
fine felt tips forming cursive
letters writing out our curses
and redemption.

Four: The Rough Edges of Sleep

The rough edges of sleep speed close
as I tumble into the mind's carpool lane.
My thoughts riding shotgun
are not composing sonnets
or rendering intricate tessellations.

Instead they wonder if my non-stick
cookware is safe. Most likely it's poisoned
the kind that would knock a parakeet dead
in my kitchen, if I had one, a parakeet that is.

A list of items I need to purchase:
Shampoo and napkins
chicken thighs and cat litter.

Ambien kicks in and I'm riding
a train now, though it gets more difficult
to remember my destination
and when and where I purchased
my ticket, and most important of all:
How does knowing any of this help me?

It's as though I've fallen from a flat
linear surface, like a page, when
most likely it's a water sport
that has me swimming
in a wavering world.
In sleep maybe everything
will make sense.

Five: Electron Fire

I string words together necklacing meaning
that can hang bright and shining
between your breasts or tight
around your neck—choked
by too close associations.

I can't predict which it will be
nor can I claim any responsibility.
It is what you've either always
craved or feared—the interpretation
is all about you.

You might see this poem
as congratulatory
in honor of your astute intellect
or as condemnation
of your critical faculties.

How can I predict
the electron fire
that will ignite in your mind
when I don't even know my own mind
as well as all that?

Life is labyrinthine
walking in circuits doubling back
the way we came to step forward
to stand full in the center
of our future that begins
in this singular moment.

We beg and plead for revelation
but there are no doves
descending to name us beloved

no public declaration
of our election
no billboards plastered
with our purpose.

And so, we leave this place
kick the dust from our sandals
bare our feet for washing
for the stooping of God
right down to our calluses.

Six: Sleep Writing

The word buzzes like live wires humming in your ears.
The word ancient as stardust settles in the soil you knead
in your hands, you crouching in buttercup and bindweed
yanking with tight fists and leather gloves, grounded in this one
moment sweat beading on your upper lip, sun beating on your back
summer sky ribboned with crows black and raucous, while all your
awareness pinpoints to this very breath and the gritty sand
underneath your kneecap crunching as you stand dizzy
with the fertility of spring, the garlic scent of weeds and subtle
perfume of tulips, heads dancing in the breeze.

Everything is listening to God singing. The song pulses in your own
wrists, thumps in your hungry belly, slips against your veiny neck.
You are the first word in the eternal story. The fruit of "let there be
light" dangles heavy from your branched heart and you divide
allegiance as day withdraws from night, but don't be afraid
of the dark, the unsaid, the prolific soil of sleep where every ordinary
thing and every common meaning is beaded in absurd fashion
and you kaleidoscope through the subterranean floors
of your self's home, damp catacombs below consciousness.

It is not Hades and you will not find Persephone's winter abode
though you long for pomegranates and sharks' sharp teeth
to amulet around your neck, while the Divine rat-a-tats along a thin
tight tendon. One might try to forget, but the skin's been seared
with symbols and words—answers and lessons and often
questions—truth inked on our very bodies.

Seven: Dream Time

There is another reality that floats like kelp
suspended below the surface of waking awareness.
Every night we gasp and dive under willingly
or we're pulled hard, mermaid latched
to the ankle, jerking us down to the shipwreck
we'd rather not encounter.

Sinking, subterranean like the drowned one
stilled from flailing, we waver in watery witness
surrender to the fluctuations of time and place
living in never-seen-before homes where we were raised
inhabiting cities and bodies unfamiliar yet ours
switching sex and setting as easy as channel surfing
becoming wholly other, wholly unrecognizable
but holy self.

I can fly all night powered only by sheer will
no wings needed to lift me from danger, simply
my chin set toward the sky, my eyes fixed
on a false ceiling as I punch through
to freedom, a lucid dreamer contributing
to the script my subconscious improvises
only to fall into sharp relief.

After twenty-five years dreamscape's sharp taste
does not dissipate. Jesus walked barefoot
across my kitchen counter through a dust
of instant pudding powder. Reaching the end
he stepped into mid-air, turned to face me
raised his arms, and hung there, in the middle

of my kitchen, fastened to invisible crossed-beams
an absurd, and I wanted to argue, unnecessary
sacrifice. I can't tell you what it means exactly
except to say he came to love me in the middle
of my messy miniscule life.

Why am I springboard diving (a holdover from high school)
dodging nets the size of sailboats meant to snare me?
What does it mean when the aquarium overflows spilling
the room with tiny tropical fish and I have no net
just my hands to scoop them to safety?

Only I can answer the questions
but not in the mornings, my mind cloudy
with dream dust, sluggish with bed glue.
So often my answer key is insufficient
and my decoder rings fail. Enigma might
be the point, but every once in a great while
a glimmer arrives delivered by carrier pigeon
alighting on my kitchen windowsill, tiny scroll
attached to its ankle while I rinse the dishes.
I pat dry my dripping hands, reach for the bird's
delicate foot, and with a single touch let loose
the mystery.

INTERCHANGES

Coming to Consciousness

For Lorraine and the November 2018 Poem a Day Group

There are mornings when the beauty outside
my window stuns me motionless. I open my eyes
to the craggy profile of Mt. Washington
rising above the Olympic Range's green ridges
and the cerulean waters of Hood Canal.

There is nothing to do but lay there
trapped under the warm weight of my blanket
listening for the growling of seals crowding
the floating platform just offshore
as I rise slowly like the slack tide
coming to consciousness an inch at a time
until I find myself fully alert.

Awake, I reach for my phone, glance at email
then scroll through my Facebook feed
because I cannot bear the bad news coming
from anyone other than my friends
who fill my screen with doom and gloom.
Instead of waking to glory I've woken to a fog
obscuring every good thing that glitters.

Preposterous circumstances and power
hungry pretenders appear to ransack
all that is good and holy and even mediocre.
My sunny attitude turns as grim as the smoky
summer mornings when I could see no further
than ash coated glass, breathing
the remains of a forest as burnt and barren

as I feel every day I don't hide from the news.

I long for those blissful moments of dreamless sleep
before I wake and begin the daily ritual of worry:
How long can this country and this planet
withstand this pillage and plunder?
I have no answer, only the weight of culpability.
The world is imploding, exploding, blazing with fury
as I slide my ballot into the collection box
an exercise in democracy that feels as effective
as extinguishing a wall of flames
with a single sneeze.

HOLY WEEK

It's time to walk tenderly
along the rutted road
dusty bare feet blistered
trouble plodding doggedly
at your heels

When hope is all that remains
and your palms are rope-burned red
make of faith and doubt
a lifeline, not a noose
and grasp tight despite the pain

Gather up grief and despair
lay them in baskets
woven from reed and tears
then lay your woes
before the one who
will not stay entombed

Build an altar
caged by ribs
for the one who animates
your every breath
from birth to death
who soon (all too soon)
will cradle you home

BUILD US A WALL FOR WAILING

Build us a wall for wailing—
make it of the mud from the fields slapped
from our soiled jeans and scraped from our nails
and shaken from our shoes with every step
taken where we were unwelcome.

And mix that mud and soil and dirt and dust
with the pesticide-laden sweat of our brows
and water it with tears for every hole barbed-wire
has punctured in our families and color it
with the blood shed by every person made illegal
every human shot in political crosshairs.

And with that soil and dirt and dust and mud
and with our sweat and tears and blood
fashion bricks to build our Wailing Wall.
Make it sturdy enough to withstand despair
wide enough to contain all longing
long enough to have no beginning or end.

Then stand before our Wailing Wall with folded
hopes and flattened dreams. Slip them into cracks
and seams. Our less than perfect offerings are how
the light gets in. Each slab and stone will crumble
when our shovels strike, pounding mud to dust
and dirt to ash to plumes rising from the ground
inhaled by the breath that formed us.

Lament for Blackfish

For the endangered Southern Resident Killer Whales

I could pilfer some prose from Carl Sagan, his pale blue
dot and grainy mote of dust suspended in a sunbeam—
and squeeze those cosmic thoughts to the smaller scale
of Puget Sound where the killer whales near extinction.

I could tell you every fact I've ever learned
about the Southern Resident orcas in the seven years
I've lived along their shores. How they're starving
at our hands that've dammed rivers and decimated wild
salmon runs; how we pump hatchery fish with antibiotics
and send them swimming into the Salish Sea—a toxic stew
of fertilizer, grease, industrial waste, and sewage.

I could offer arguments like a *Seattle Times'* editorial.
Tell you an entire generation was herded into coves
and kidnapped, sold into slavery, forced to live and die
in concrete tanks performing circus tricks for spectators
like me who flocked to SeaWorld, sat in the splash zone
and cheered before I knew better.

I'd want you to know the clan's matriarch, Granny, died
at the impossible age of 105 and since she disappeared
her pods split ever smaller to forage often fruitlessly
for fish. That only seventy-four family members remain.
That two on the verge of starvation will certainly sink
into the sea come summer.

I'd want you to know this because twenty years ago
I bobbed in a tour boat off the San Juan Islands

and a dorsal fin knifed the water at our bow
accompanied by an exhale as forceful as a hundred
tired men and I gazed into the orca's black eye
as he watched me. I've heard their voices on hydrophones
broadcast on my computer speakers. Sharp squeals
and squeaks that disturb my cats, insistent cries
that can't be ignored. I've spotted them through binoculars
surfacing, fin slapping, even sleeping in waters
off Seattle's shore.

And now, some nights they swim into my dreams.
Breaching in the too shallow bays outside my home
swimming upriver alongside my car as I drive
winding forest roads. Native tribes believe Blackfish
were once people who shed their skins and took to the sea.
What does my family need, and who can help us?

Like Lady Macbeth, blood stains my hands, and I wring
my wrists in worry. How can I put an end to PCB's
and plastics? How can I reverse overfishing and under-caring?
How can I stop the Navy's sonar blasts
and SeaWorld in its money-grubbing tracks?

If I were brave, I'd fight for their survival
slice salmon free from fisherman's nets
blow up the Snake River dams
scale an electrified fence and set captive Lolita free.
But I am a nothing more than a coward with a pen
caught in a lurching stagger toward the sea
where I drop to my knees and keen a useless
lament as stars explode and orcas sing.

HOWL WITH THE EARTH

For Sharon Daloz Parks

Carry us to the wounded belly of Love
and cradle those whose innocence and
safety and choice have been destroyed.

Lift us to the open ears of Mercy and hear
the groans of all who are voiceless.

Set us to weeping for those
who do not have the luxury of tears.

Teach us to wail and howl with the earth and all her
creatures whose voices we have not yet learned to hear.

Rip off the masks of our privilege and competence
our expertise and lethargy.
Strip us of hopelessness and excuses.

Embrace us and enlarge our insufficient metaphors
so that teetering here on the precipice, we might bridge
the chasm of the lie of separation—and hold the deep
heartbreak that is no stranger, but sister
and kiss the face of fear who is none other than brother.

Let us listen until all our walls are broken down
listen until the wild colts and skittish ponies
of our spirits still their frantic struggle and begin
to trust, taking tentative steps away
from the security and prison of our stalls.

Incline our hearts and our hearing and our hoarse
underused voices toward healing and tune us
toward humble listening, toward trustworthy speech
and bold prophecy as you serenade us ever closer
to the beauty-soaked edges of truth.

Deliver us to the words beneath words
that we might rise free from every false division
and together soar—a flock of wild winged ones
taking flight in this very breath.

ERUPTION

For Kate & David

A photo of Kilauea erupting hangs above
the dining table. In the image unmistakable
faces float in smoke, specters etched
in ashy plumes rising high into the sky.

Kate and David enjoyed a life
of sweet aloha until molten lava
leveled their neighborhood, their house.
Before the immolation they spent
glowing evenings skirting the spectacle
from the safety of their truck.

One clear night, Pele, legendary
Goddess of Fire who shapes
the sacred landscape appeared
before them wearing white
walking atop the roiling ruby flow
as if out for a simple stroll
with her white dog following
placid at her heels.

In the instant it took Kate and David
to turn toward each other and blink
both Goddess and canine evaporated
leaving no trace of themselves among
the devastation, but memory renders
the terrible beauty of that night
more vivid than any photograph.

BLACK OVER FIRE

A response to Tarah Trueblood's painting

"Be careful," our parents pled.
"Safety first," our teachers said.
Take Shelter, the signs read.

If they believed we belonged secure inside
these solid walls, sequestered, ensconced
then who were we to doubt?

It's not difficult to turn the deadbolt
in its lock, to draw the curtains closed
and block out the wild world.

But deep down the soul
never stops smoldering.

All it takes is a pinprick for light
to pierce the dark and a single spark
can ignite obsidian black

with flaming fringes and fiery tongues
that skirt the halls and scale the walls
until the blaze, emboldened

batters down the door
and all restraints are shattered.

Then the world's gone molten
life exploding everywhere
like seeds once dormant
finally free to grow.

DETOURS

WALKING THE TIGHTROPE

I'd like to pen a lively literate alliteration of the current situation
an artful arrangement of carefully crafted curses silky as
Shakespearean sleeves and sharp barded barbs beaded between
banter laid like lane lines restriping our route on the interstate
to the unthinkable.

I turn to traffic mitigation, tendering flashing neon arrows
and orange cones. I litter the landscape with impact attenuators
and Do Not Enter spikes designed to puncture hot air from the daily
deluge of blowhard barrage threatening to flatten us like road-kill
devour us like carrion.

All around the prophets intone, and we must atone, retreat, repent
reverse our trajectory at warp speed and flap furiously away from
the furnace like the proverbial bats out of hell. Contrary to popular
opinion, ostriches do not bury their heads in the sand, they dig
instead safe nests for their offspring. And likewise, echolocation
does not simply serve to avoid obstacles, but penetrates our very
bodies with waves that vibrate the truth not in our ears, but straight
through our jaws.

We teeter on the edge of the has-been and the yet-to-come, our
ballast and balance nothing more than a ballot and a ballpoint pen
poised to close the chasm. The pen's nib, its spider thread of thin
black ink becomes the tightrope on which we'll step—boldly
I hope—into our future.

BREAK HERE NOW

A poet friend
once cautioned me
against short lines
he said they
lacked the gravity
and certain sincerity
serious poetry requires.

He was convinced
that the eye wants to
roam wide across pages
gathering up meaning
like bundled wheat
with sweeping gazes
across inked prairies
and billowing clouds
stretched thin as worn
sheets before the reader
slows her attention
patiently, gleaning
after a harvest
each black syllable
a satisfying morsel
before the taught
line breaks.

Not so now
this short line
the eye skims
with quick flick

sharp swift glance
three words here
three more there
in quick cascade
ruby slippers clicking
in downward descent
rushing the staircase
in mad dash
to answer
the ringing bell
and insistent knock
of a lover
she once knew
at the door
flung open wide.

Up she flew off the page
breeze filled balloon
attempting escape
after the panic
the line grounded
the fire doused
her slippers clicked
three times fast
brought her home
walking the lane
toward Auntie Em
and Uncle Henry
past a rusty
red wheelbarrow
that once belonged
to William Carlos Williams
and his line break
upon which
so much depended.

For Our Hunger

a chicken
a guitar
a vase
me

We each
in turn
will be taken
by the neck
and

plucked
strummed
filled
wrung

And (sadly)
in the end
broken

but not before
we offer
(I hope)
our little morsel
to this world

a meal
a melody
a bouquet
a poem

GUIDED MEDITATION

I imagine a dappled meadow on a bright blue afternoon
breeze rustling my bangs, a brook babbling
butterflies flitting, my mind a blank sky-sheet
muscles milky and soft, a dreamless semi-state
from which I'll float seamlessly into the demands
of day. I will be chipper, unflappable
infinitely patient and kind, a model of mystic mojo.

But my mind manufactures a plaid picnic blanket
and three-layer cake, coconut frosting gone gooey
in the sun. I sit lotus-legged craving the cake yet
simply notice my desire then let it flit by.

An army of ants advances through the grass.
I offer no resistance, no flicking with forefinger
no breaking their offensive line. But, I wonder
why no curious ant steps out of formation to spy
what's ahead. Instead, she stares at her cousin's rump.

I miss my cousins. It's been too long. Really, they're
my mother's cousins. Should I call them second or
once-removed? I was never much for relational
mapping. But these cousins, whatever their
nomenclature, are the only ones I've met.

The ants swarm and gorge on my coconut cake
before heading for home to some subterranean farm
carrying Mount-Rushmore-sized crumbs on their backs.

It would flatten me, lifting ten, twenty, fifty times
my body weight: a Dodge Caravan filled with five

gymnasts I'll cart home chalked and sweaty
after their workout to celebrate my daughter's birthday.
I will squish thirteen candles into a nine-by-thirteen cake
baked from box mix topped with tubbed frosting.

There will be no cousins and no ants, just the babbling
of pubescent girls who'll squeal and thump
through the house, leaping wild with imagination
landing plumb center in my heart.

I will want to swaddle them in a plaid blanket
cradled close to my bones and gaze
on their dappled cheeks
each one eternal as the sun.

VOYAGE OF DISCOVERY

For Chrissy

I was wearing my ratty nightgown wiping toothpaste
from my mouth when you stood in the bathroom door
fingers tucked deep into the pockets of your jeans
and said with a shrug *I like him, a lot.*

And now, instead of you and me slung across the couch
on Friday nights with a DVD in the player and purring cats
in our laps, it's the two of you bolted to attention while I pad
around the kitchen until I run out of contrived chores
leaving you alone together.

There you are, the Lewis and Clark of the living room
tracing paths across each other's fleshy limbs. You, who
used to love *101 Dalmatians* and turning cartwheels on the lawn.
You, and this boy I hardly know, map uncharted territory
like Columbus, or better yet, one of his ships.

The Santa Maria kissing over waves across the Atlantic
rounding the cusp of the sea as if no one ever fell off the edge.
Naked strangers in a new world, you and he, the sole inhabitants
of Paradise. Adam and Eve pitched in a garden dripping with fruit
not even a serpent slithering at your feet to warn you—just me,
who pushed you blue and slippery into being, the mother who
used to be your God—and I fall upon the original language:

Oh honey, anything but the apple.

DAILY I FALL IN LOVE WITH THE DEMOLITION CREW

After "Daily I Fall in Love with Waitresses" by Elliot Fried

Daily I fall in love with the demolition crew
with their white dust masks
and steel-toed boots.
I love how they bend
over sheetrock sweeping debris.
Their flannel shirts
unbuttoned above toolbelts
t-shirts peeking out below
collars like Mt. Rainier—
a frozen volcano wrapped in clouds.
I feel their fingers
calloused inside their nitrile gloves
rip down my dilapidated house.
Their biceps and well-used bodies
keep moving so…
pounding and ripping so seamlessly
that I am left gaping.
Daily I fall in love with the demolition crew
with their can-do deconstruction.
They tell jokes by the dump truck
and I want in on them.
They carry plywood, posts, nails, concrete
their legs are crowbar strong.

They are tear-it-down tricky—
they know how tiles crack.
Their nimble fingers expose electric wires
and rust-pocked plumbing.

Daily I fall in love with the demolition crew.
They strike sledgehammer inspiration
but they never stand still long enough
as they wreck, wreck, wreck.

DISTURBING THE PEACE

For Suzanne Seaton

My mind is a bad neighborhood at 2 a.m.
Worry prowls the streets like a thug
intent on trouble hurling rocks through windows
shattering illusions that tumble to rubble.
Fear joins the fray, reveling in ruckus turned to riot.

Panic, frantic for help, dials 911but there's no
squad car on scene to silence the what-if gang
no patrol cop to arrest the worst-case-scenario
masterminds, no helicopter shining a searchlight
in dark alleys, revealing dread hidden and trembling
behind a dumpster.

Pulse pounding, hands shaking, Faith manages
to crack open the door, and in the slim sliver
of moonlight I spot Jesus scrawling "Surrender"
across the sky. I step onto the porch as he lands
broom in hand, smack into the chaos of my life.
He starts sweeping—back and forth, back and forth—
humming in time with the scritching bristles.

He tsks terror to the gutter—nothing now
but harmless heaps of nonattachment— and whisks
his way toward me feet kissing the sidewalk.

I watch and breathe, watch and breathe
as he draws near, peace perfuming his heels.
"You know," he says to me, "we're all Buddhists
in the middle of the night."

EVERYTHING IS WAITING FOR YOU

With apologies to David Whyte

Everything is waiting for you
well, almost everything is waiting
well, maybe almost everything
well, if not everything than
definitely something
certainly something is waiting
more than likely something
probably something, hopefully something
maybe something is waiting…

Truthfully, it's doubtful there's something
…there might have been something
waiting for you once…a very long time ago
but it's gone now run off with the ghost of something
or other haunting the temple of somebody's
familiar that no one ever gave you directions to.

And now there's nothing, and I mean nothing
and now there's nothing, and I mean nothing
and now there's nothing, and I mean nothing—
except this unnecessary repetition
that you would've noticed right off
if you'd been listening, if you'd been
paying attention like you're supposed to.

Seriously, all that's waiting for you
is the vast void of infinite interconnected
and eternal nothingness.
Have fun with that.

PHILOSOPHY FOR THE VOCABULARY IMPAIRED

Is that *all* there is?

All is there.
All is that.
There is that.
There it is.

Is *there* all that is?

There is all that is.
All that is, there is.
All is there, that is.

It, there. Is *that* all?

Yes.

SCENIC ROUTES

WEATHER REPORT

The blue is too bright today
the sky relentlessly sunny and sharp.
The high of 78 will exacerbate your hangover
so sit in the shade and pull your sunglasses
over your bloodshot eyes.

Hold your head still so that the breeze
blowing in from the southwest
at seven miles an hour won't further parch
your cotton mouth and sandpaper eyes.

Sip something ice-cold
and hold the weeping glass against
your flaming cheeks and neck—
which should be hung in shame
in preparation for the storm brewing
inside the kitchen where your lover
slams doors and cabinet drawers
as though a temblor
from the San Andreas Fault
is shaking the very foundation
of your life.

Yes, the sun is glaring—
all your errors in sharp relief
no cloud cover to hide behind.
Duck, I tell you because today
the shit's finally going to hit the fan.

ALUMINUM SKIES

My father asks how I—a recent California transplant—like living
in *the land of aluminum skies*, under the misapprehension
that in the Pacific Northwest our view is always veiled—
monochromatic gray the shade of desiccated liver.

The skyscape kaleidoscopes all day in Puget Sound.
Clouds pour like lava, layer into thundering club sandwiches
of pewter and steel, pigeon and dove, dolphin and trout
then tumble into wadded white sheets dulled by cold
water washes, then taffy-stretch thin, loose gauzy layers
of pearl pantyhose bunched around God's ankles.

And the blue, when it's here, always looks enhanced
too dramatic to be real. Royal, azure, and cerulean
dazzling iris and sapphire, cornflower and cobalt
powerful and intense, relentless as the gaze it commands.

Sunsets scald crimson and claret, blood and burnt orange
fire and fuchsia in ribbed tongues. Clouds sear into charcoal
flames then to embers as the Sound stills shimmering flamingo pink
with civil twilight dissolving into ash on our tongues. Blinded
by beauty we are left to navigate nightfall by Braille the jagged
peaks of the Olympics and Cascades framing the horizon.

Each night a burnt offering, each dawn a blessing
in the land of aluminum sky.

As Time and Tides Converge

The stars in the sky shimmer
like oyster shells beneath your feet
the sharp, cold, stings of home
ebb as you walk the beach
feet crunching against
the rocky expanse at low tide
reflected light exposing starfish
and urchins that usually sleep
undetected underwater.

You keep watch for them
vulnerable as they are
treading round them with care
patient as the moon
who wanes and waxes
in ancient rhythms
and conjures a flood tide
that baptizes you
in this sea that birthed
and claims you.

IN PRAISE OF THE NATURE POET

The nature poet lifts his hand
like a conductor, a gentle pulse
emphasizing each distinct syllable
his fist closed, but loose
as if each thing he has described—

the delicate-winged moth
the striated canyon slopes
the mossy emerald forest
the sharp-taloned hawk—
is cradled in his own sweet palm.

Geography and geology
flora and fauna, class and phyla
endangered and common—
he incarnates entire kingdoms
from nothing but words
and fertile imagination
sheltered and safeguarded
by his touch.

How I want to reach for this wizard's hand
how I want to unfurl his green-leafed fingers
and reveal the roots of his golden touch—
the hand a wand, the mouth an oracle
the poem a portal, a blazing perfect gift.

In Flight

The 737 lifts off over volcanic cones of the Cascades
and hulking Mt. Rainier looms into view as we climb
to 10,000 feet then disappears as we bank west
hurtling above the Coastal Range's jagged green
teeth biting from Washington to Oregon to California.
Rivers run like molten silver as our metal box reflects
the sun's flames along their courses.

At 38,000 feet the Pacific bleeds into the horizon
and my thoughts slip from the microscope
of daily concerns to a cosmic perspective
though I see only a small sliver of creation—
one ruffled edge of a single continent
fringed by sand and foam a landscape dotted by lakes
rivers, roads, forests, fields, and settlements.

The dancing plumes of forest fire smoke float
over ridgetops like low hung clouds. From this
perspective even destruction looks serene.

While I gaze out the window my seatmates watch
videos on their phones. I'm flying to the side
of one soon to die. What else will I see upon
landing? This world, our lives, are bathed
in both brokenness and glory—the all of it
achingly beautiful.

WALKING HIGHWAY 106

My hiking boots pad along the asphalt
a rhythmic and steady thwap accompanied
by the swish of my arms swinging
in my stiff coat and the tinny twang
of my zipper head rattling against
the snap as my legs stretch forward.

I step onto the shoulder, gravel crackling
under my feet as I make way
for vehicles that whoosh, engines throbbing
tires rumbling toward me from both directions
droning that peaks then recedes as one
after another, school bus, pickup, SUV, speed by.

In the quiet gaps between cars I hear
water flume down the steep hillside
tumbling forceful as waterfalls
through open-troughed pipes
into drainage ditches sluicing roadside.

Below the armored embankment, waters
of Anna's Bay glug and gurgle against the shore
tide rising to cover the stink of rotting marine life
and sea grass uncovered in the morning's ebb.

An unseen eagle utters its stuttering cry
somewhere amid the evergreens towering above—
high pitched staccato that belies its commanding
appearance. The tiny belted kingfisher ricochets
from power line to cedar to pier piling
with voice bursting loud like rapid fire bullets.

Seagulls float in the water ar-ar-ar-guing
their squawking frantic, insistent, grating.

After a mile I turn toward home
stopping every few yards to stoop and gather
discarded beers cans and soda bottles, crushed
lighters and water-logged plastic bags.

The sun slants low in the sky
illuminating everything.

AT FAYE BAINBRIDGE PARK

I pick my way along the trunks of trees
bleached like bones and strewn upon the beach.
Jumping from one relic to the next I forge
a wooden path over rocks and seaweed
and think what it took to topple these
once proud and stately firs, cedars, elms.

What forces must have cleaved them
from familiar earth, uprooted them from home
and swept them into the sea rolling and pitching
until—who knows how many months or years later—
a king tide delivered them tempest tossed
and waterlogged to this shore.

I wonder how long they will stay
horizontal in this haven, if like heaven
forever, or if some epic wave will crash
in and buoy them away to another coastline
where they will once again lie down in surrender—
their reaching past and branching dreams
nothing but a watery memory, fleeting
as the last slice of sun on the horizon.

What If People Dropped Like Leaves?

What if people dropped like leaves
our last months and days a dazzling display
brilliant reds, yellows, orange flaming
bodies, a glorious glow
that draws others from miles around
to gaze in amazement eyes wide in wonder—
remembering how we began so plain
young, green, ordinary, unremarkable
and near our end—blazing beauty
stunning shimmering shadows in the sun's
low arc across autumn skies

This should be how one dies—
a grand metamorphosis
waving brilliant
until with one simple move
we let go of everything
that binds us
and leaf-thin float free
in silent descent, graceful and spent
released from achievements
and attachments, family trees and branches
until we come to rest at last
in the loam of the gloaming

FRESH PAVEMENT

HOW TO SPEAK YOUR TRUTH

To say what will not be
coaxed from the lips
one must reach deep
into the green-
throated past
memory grown thick
as jungle weed.
One must wield
the Hori knife
against the strangling vines
and slowly, carefully
cut away the once small
once innocent tendrils
grown thick with secrets
revealing the body
it hides until the voice
flutters free climbing
on lace leafed wings
far above the branching
family tree and the debris
now heaped at its feet.

SMALL CHANGES

I'd hop the express train to transformation
if it were that simple—pawn my minivan
hire a Sherpa, sit at a guru's feet
on a jagged peak drinking locust tea
all for a glimpse of enlightenment
a glowing horizon of serenity—
the metallic bite of suffering
faded like a forgotten photo
of someone I knew once, someone I clung to
because I thought love meant I couldn't let go
of anxiety and fear exploding like solar flares
in my mind and heart. Without their singe
how would I know I was truly alive?

But change is no grand adventure, no scroll
unfurled with trumpet herald proclaimed
before a court of admirers applauding one's
audacity. Releasing our chains resounds
with all the fanfare of feathers floating to the floor
forward progress measured in synapses, microns
and eons. It is the smallest decision departing
from past patterns made in this moment
and again, in this moment now
punctuated like so…

Do Not Be Afraid

"Do not be afraid," the angels repeat
as they beat their wings behind their backs
confronting unwed mothers, mute
and unsuspecting fathers, and future
apostles on God's behalf.

"Do not be afraid," their standard preface
to the humans who shake and sweat
in the face of the supernatural
presence before them.

My feral kitten Malika cowers under the bed
while I reach below the frame and extend
my arm, tuna-flavored treat in my open palm.
"Don't be scared," I say, "I won't hurt you."
She doesn't budge, doesn't believe.

But Mary and Joseph and Peter and Isaiah
and others like them hear angels harken
and step toward the live coal
offering their lips for scorching,
their reputations for ruining, their bodies for bearing.

They are afraid, and it will hurt, does sting
but even in their worry and doubt they assent.
I imagine myself a Mary, but my actions are
pure Malika, cowering stone. How I wish
for a hand to scruff my neck and drag me
trembling toward belief.

ONE ORDINARY NIGHT

One ordinary night an ordinary donkey bore
an immigrant mother and her unborn son
on its back to a place where there was no
room and no welcome. And yet no one
and no *thing* could stop love from breaking
into that bleak night. Breath and blood, stars
and bone—that child born became our own.

Not just that night but this night and every night
and not just there but here and in every desolate place
and homeless heart, hope—like an infant—arrives
to grasp at the smallest sliver of light and hold fast
illuminating the darkness.

FAITH

It's simple and terrifying
to let go of everything
we thought we required
to give up every expectation
to relinquish all control
as if speeding in the fast
lane no hands on the wheel

It's blind and brash to toss
the map out the window
to trust that life will not steer us
anywhere we aren't meant to go
to believe that every billboard
is a sign we're meant to read

And it's pure crazy to suspect
that a crash is just one
more instrument of surrender
but somehow I can't help it

TELL ME

...about things that cannot be explained
about the first time the world
slipped out from under your feet

I want to know
if you were dizzy if your breath held
if your heart lurched if you crashed

what did you call it
and what did it taste like
that first touch of...
that first glimpse of...
...beyond your self?

translate that numinous nothing
into words I can grasp hold of
take my hand and summon
phosphorescent angels
blazing with heavenly light
teach me their dance

invite me to feast on mystery
and make fat the sacred belly
of the universe
I'm hungry for your truth
thirsty for the pearl in your palm
speak to me of love
we're all listening for God

MAGNUM OPUS

Every day the divine composes your score.
Your body, your bones, your marrow are measured.
Your breath flows in whole notes and quarters
in rests, in sharps, and flats.
Your accordion lungs, snare drum heart
cello kidneys, all play in acoustic trio.
Your mouth a flute, your blood a concerto.

Each movement, each platelet and modulation
marked, magnificent as the spleen, efficient
as the central nervous system synapsing
a cantata transmitted by telegraph line
a hymn ringing over high-spined mountains
spanning rivers, spilling lymph and bile
spit and sweat into the echoing ocean.

The infinite orchestrates each movement
your cells an ensemble multiplying and dividing
in crescendo at dizzying speeds, forgetting
everything but harmony and rhythm.

Each morning the sky explodes
with golden-fugued fire and the world is sparked
into melody, each body sliding from sleep in glissando
joining the symphony. The metronome ticks
the conductor's baton pierces your heart:
You stand upright and sing.

HEADING HOME

SUMMER 1971

The radio blares over speakers
at the community pool where
lifeguards tower over us, tan gods
in mirrored sunglasses and red swim trunks
whistles dangling around necks I clung
to at five, six, seven. Ten now, with bikini
knotted at bony hips, I'm pulled under
water as much by the lament Carole King
croons as by my best friend's ankle tug
into three-foot shallows where
cross-legged we bubble out lyrics
until lungs empty of air and we surface
gasping, blinking chlorine.

We haul out like seals shivering and wet
on cement, sun kissing skin, until revived
we trot toward the diving board, wait
in the dripping line while kids bounce
cannonball, splash to commercial jingles.
We're impatient for a real song—inspiration
for the head-long plunge into twelve-foot
water—leaping lungs fortified by one huge
gulp before we rocket into the deep
touch bottom, then turn and kick hard
hands clasped straight above our heads
pointing like arrows toward the waiting world.

BLESSED

For Jennifer. After Stephen Kuusisto's "Café Solo with an Old Horn"

Jesus, what were you thinking?
I'm the one who sacrificed her life.
Move over Martha Stewart—
I invented homemaking.

Motherhood's littered with soiled diapers
and snot-trailed clothes
but my husband is faithful
the car runs and the children
are fully alive, bellies rising in sleep.
Of course, you can see God
in their eyes.

In the spring I plant tomatoes.
My toddler in Batman cape
raking behind me stops suddenly
points at the blue above us
amazed. The moon round and white
floats in the afternoon sky.

When she holds my hand
I remember how love began.

ASH WEDNESDAY REPENTANCE

For My Father

It's been seven years since my father and I
have graced a room together, and never
once have I sat at his feet, not even as a child,
until tonight when I hear his confession,
rise from my place on the leather couch,
cross the floor to his antique chair, kneel
and reach for his hands that grip mine tight.

Unexpected, unbidden these words he offers me
against the backdrop of HGTV, repentance
for wrongs long ago committed, apologies
for harm his failings have caused.

Surely the sins of our fathers and our mothers
have visited each of us in severity and turn.

But what my father retrieves from ashes
and dust this night is not confession's sackcloth
nor hair shirt of penitence but words of love.

For it is love's remains smeared across
our souls, its charred stains that linger
long after worldly success has blown
away like chaff and health has begun
its inevitable decline and we become
nothing but remembrance and bones.

On this night of ash and intention we repent
of everything that's kept us distant.
I am claimed and marked by one who created me

one who has both known and caused suffering—
released to the holy now by his benediction:

"If you remember anything, remember that I've
always loved you and that I always will."

Later, I retire to his guest room, slide into bed
and cross my forehead with my thumb—
the burnt embers of honesty
seared there by my father's kiss.
I understand it now, how the truth
can set you free, how it becomes a path
unmistakable, no matter how faint. Our
footfalls smudge over the hills and valleys
of life, releasing the past to float away
in a cloud of dust yoking us
to one another as we step ever closer
to love's fiery pillar.

SLOW DANCING

For Kevin, with thanks to musician Craig Cardiff, and hosts Pam & Jerry

Slow dancing with my husband
in the kitchen at the house concert
our hosts' refrigerator hums
accompanying the soft-spoken
singer strumming his guitar.
We corkscrew between counters
laden with wine and cheese
hot dogs, chips, and dip—my
husband's clasped hands folding
the small of my back close.
Our feet sweep the tile while
the songwriter repeats his refrain
"The lions go back to their cages."

Bellies filled with deli snacks
bodies swaying in unison
we compass small circles
in time to the Canadian's crooning
acting like lions who've never
struck with shear-sharp claws
never disturbed our pride
with bellows and roars
never sunk our teeth
into another's skin
never stolen a kill.

The singer tames his feral
audience back into captivity.

We applaud, and I slink to my bar
stool leg pressed the length
of my husband's thigh
awaiting the next song
in the ringmaster's set.

We may all be confined to cages
but sometimes the world is kind
sometimes the bars are set wide
and sometimes the twilight sky
is tinged with love poems.

KNIT IN JOY

Faith is the wheel
that travels the true road
you and I spin together.

Hands clasped, destinies linked
we grasp the future outstretched
and cradle the fresh-birthed self.

Imagination binds us in possibility
hope strewn like jewels under our feet
a benediction knit in joy.

Wide-eyed we circle the sun
and everywhere love
spills from our open mouths.

HOME BY ANOTHER ROAD

For Kevin, Becky, and Tarah

I can't tell you how it happens
except to say it does—
gradually often imperceptibly
until resting on the far side
we turn back to peer into the tunnel—
cramped, damp, foreboding—
from which we've emerged.

Between hard place and rock
we somehow squeeze through—
scraping across years inches
at a time, until we crawl free
a bit bloody, but wiser, kinder
braver than we thought possible.

We are not the same ones
who set out so long ago
innocent and unscathed.
Train wrecks and trauma
cancer and crashed economies
divorce, despair, and death—
familiar foes are shot through
the beautiful broken lives we lead.

And yet look at us, here we still are
walking home by another road
carrying the mended shards of dreams
in astounding new configurations.
Your resilience is pure miracle—

and if I believe in anything
I believe because of you
who still love—despite everything.

ACKNOWLEDGMENTS

Most of these poems materialized in the Pacific Northwest in the five years after the publication of *Burnt Offerings* (January 2014)– just two years after my husband and I moved to a fixer-upper on Bainbridge Island from California's Santa Cruz Mountains. Since then, we've lived in three more fixers (each in a different town), and I've become a real estate broker, in addition to remodeling houses with our Yellow Ribbon Homes crew. I hold a shop vac as often as a pen, and am delighted to have created a new book from sporadic musings.

Home By Another Road wouldn't exist without Peggy Rosenthal's manuscript advice, and the contributions of many who've written (in-person and virtually) with and inspired me.

Lucy Dickinson, Daniel Love, Elizabeth Eisenhoodl, Patty Molloy, Marty Steyer, and Georgann Turner created beauty in my Bainbridge Island Holy Ink Spiritual Writing workshop. "Welcome" and "Tell Me," were originally written for them. Constance Mears and Carey Taylor spilled Holy Ink in my Manchester living room overlooking Puget Sound. Danielle Cruver, Clara Sciortino, and Molly Viers graced my Writing for Renewal class at Gig Harbor's Tacoma Community College branch. I wrote "Weather Report," "That Old Coat," and "The Imposter" with them.

I raise a glass to Jerry Libstaff who welcomed me into Watermark Writers, his labor of love on the Key Peninsula. Jerry organized monthly readings with regional poets at Gig Harbor's Morso wine bar—where I was honored to be a featured reader, and where a featured reader inspired "In Praise of the Nature Poet"—a monthly open mike at The Blend wine shop, a weekly writing group, and a seasonal concert series where "Slow Dancing," came to life. Thank you, Jerry, for the opportunity to soak up words penned by you, Carolyn Wiley, Linda Whaley, Irene Torres, Linda Arrington, Dale Godvin, Gayle Slaten, Carrie Schiffler, Jan Eamon, and Lorraine Hart. Lorraine delivers amazing poetry prompts each November day and inspired "Coming to Consciousness," "Walking the Tightrope," "Small Changes," and "Walking Highway 106."

The Upper Room's Greater Northwest Five Day Academy for Spiritual Formation is a crucible for my faith and creativity. I'm deeply grateful to organizers Roberta Egli, Denise McGuiness, Sue Magrath, Juli and David Reinholz, Louie Jones, Pat Rankin, and Charlotte Cordner; presenters Suzanne Seaton, Paul Jeffrey, Sharon Daloz Parks, and Cynthia Wilson; and those in my covenant groups. "As Time and Tides Converge," "A Lament for the Severed One," "Build Us a Wall for Wailing," "Howl with the Earth," "Disturbing the Peace," and "Everything Is Waiting for You," were birthed during two sessions at the Academy.

Several artists selected my poems in the annual Ars Poetica art-poetry pairing on the Kitsap Peninsula. My gratitude to: Assemblage artist Steve Parmelee who constructed the snare drum heart from "Magnum Opus"; Bill Walcott, painter, for his faithful rendering of, "At Faye Bainbridge State Park"; printmaker Paula Gill who learned a new woodblock technique for "Aluminum Skies"; Michelle Van Berkom for her watercolor "What If People Fell Like Leaves"; and Michelle Purdue who portrayed "As Time and Tides Converge" with digital media.

Two of my poems are interpretations of Tarah Trueblood's art. Her painting "Black Over Fire" (which became the cover art for *Burnt Offerings*) inspired the poem of the same name. And "Knit in Joy" is my response to her drawing #HopeLooksLike.

I'm grateful to the congregation at Boulder Creek (CA) United Methodist Church where I was nurtured in the infancy of both my faith and writing and where I penned, "Crazy Along Highway 9," "Avalanche," and "Eclipsed." Twenty years later, I worship at St. David of Wales Episcopal Church in Shelton (WA). Fittingly, St. David is the Patron Saint of Poets, and I often slip poetry into the weekly bulletins. Thank you, Rev. Joseph Mikel (now retired) and fellow parishioners. "One Ordinary Night" is for you.

To my husband Kevin, daughters Jennifer and Chrislynn, and soul sisters Becky and Tarah, who sustain and enrich this journey: I offer my deepest love and awe.

And finally, thank you, dear reader for reading these words— may they, in some small way, bless you.

Cathy Warner
Union, Washington
February 14, 2019

CATHY WARNER is a poet, writer, teacher, editor, home renovator, and real estate broker who lives with her husband and cats in a fixer-upper on the shores of Washington's Hood Canal—and is never far from her camera and binoculars. Her books include *Home By Another Road* and *Burnt Offerings*. Cathy's fiction, short memoir, and essays have appeared in dozens of print journals and online venues including *Under the Sun, Tell Us a Story, The Other Journal, So To Speak, Water~Stone,* and the blogs of *Ruminate, Relief,* and *Image.* She's published in several anthologies, most recently *West of the Divide.* Recipient of the Steinbeck and SuRaa fiction awards, Cathy has been nominated for the Pushcart Prize and Best American Essays. Find her photo-haikus, blog, audio poetry, and more at cathywarner.com.

Made in the USA
Lexington, KY
07 November 2019